JOHN LENNON

NOWHERE BOY

A film by Sam Taylor-Wood

LEVEL

SCHOLASTIC

Adapted by: Paul Shipton

Publisher: Jacquie Bloese

Editor: Tanya Whatling

Designer: Mo Choy

Picture research: Pupak Navabpour

Photo credits:
Page 5: Picture Post/Getty Images; P Lomas/Rex Features.
Page 12: J Hamilton/Rex Features.
Pages 78 & 79: M Ochs, Redferns/Getty Images; Pictorial Press/Alamy.
Pages 80 & 81: AP/Topham; SSPL/Manchester Daily Express/ Getty Images; H Lamb/BEI/Rex Features.
Pages 82 & 83: P Libera/Corbis; M Harrison/AFP/Getty Images; P Thomas/Press Association Images; The Image Works/Topfoto.

Impressão e acabamento: Gráfica Eskenazi
Lote: 294765

Published by Scholastic Ltd. 2011

Mary Glasgow Magazines (Scholastic Ltd)
Euston House
24 Eversholt Street
London NW1 1DB

Printed in Brazil
2021

Contents

JOHN LENNON is sixteen years old. He lives in Liverpool with his aunt and uncle. He goes to a good school, but he is always in trouble there. His teachers say that he is going nowhere. John has other ideas.

MIMI is John's aunt. She has looked after him since he was a little boy. Order and appearances are very important to her.

GEORGE is Mimi's husband and is very different from Mimi. He is friendly and funny. John can relax with his uncle.

JULIA is Mimi's younger sister and John's real mother. John hasn't seen her for a long time. He learns that she still lives close to Mimi's house.

PAUL McCARTNEY, like John, is a teenager from Liverpool with dreams of rock 'n' roll. He can play the guitar and sing really well, and he is already ambitious for the future.

PETE is John's best friend from school. They do everything together. He joins John's first band, although he isn't so interested in music.

PLACES

LIVERPOOL is a large city on the coast in the north west of England. In the 1950s many ships from the US arrived in Liverpool and so people in the city heard new rock 'n' roll records before other people in the UK.

WOOLTON is an area of Liverpool, to the south of the city. Many of the houses there are quite large and expensive.

BLACKPOOL is a seaside town not far from Liverpool. In the 1950s it was a popular place to go for day trips or on longer holidays.

JOHN LENNON
NOWHERE BOY

CHAPTER 1
'Glasses, John!'

John was running.

He was wearing his school uniform and he was running as fast as he could past the stone entrance of one of the grand old buildings in Liverpool's city centre. He looked quickly over one shoulder. There was nobody behind him, but he could hear them – hundreds, thousands *of people – and they were all shouting and screaming for him. John laughed as he ran down the steps. He had never felt so alive.*

'John! John!'

John's eyes opened to early morning light. His aunt was standing over his bed, and as usual she did not look happy.

'Do I ignore you?' Mimi said. There was a note of anger in her voice. 'No. So please do not ignore me. I have called you twice. Now hurry up or you'll be late for school.' She sighed and left the room. School … . School wasn't one of John's favourite places.

Fifteen minutes later, he was dressed and sitting at the breakfast table alone with the newspaper. The room was extremely tidy. Everything had its place. John had never seen newspapers on the floor, or dirty plates left on the table. Aunt Mimi liked order.

John looked up from his paper as Uncle George walked in, singing to himself as he always did in the mornings. He pulled something from his pocket and placed it in front of John – a shiny, new harmonica.

George nodded at the instrument. 'Very expensive,' he said.

'Really?'

'No.'

They both laughed.

George moved closer. 'First lesson – tonight, eight o'clock. Don't be late.'

John reached over the table and gave his uncle a hug. It was easy to have fun with his uncle. He wished it could be the same with his aunt.

John looked up at the clock: his friend Pete was probably outside the house already. Every day before school, Pete came to call for him on his bike. As John pushed his own bicycle out, he heard a knock from the front window. He knew why. Every day, they followed the same routine. He turned. Mimi was standing there; she made circles with her fingers and thumbs and held them up to her eyes.

'Glasses, John!' she shouted.

'Glasses, John!' repeated Pete with a laugh.

John hated wearing glasses, but he took them out of his pocket and put them on. As soon as they were around the next corner, he took his glasses off again. He wondered if Mimi knew that.

Outside the house, John was a different person. He was always ready with a joke, and if a joke hurt someone's feelings, that wasn't his problem. As he and Pete cycled on, they rode past three older boys from their school. One of them was taller and heavier than his two friends.

'Oy, you!' John shouted to him. 'Keep out of the chip shop!'

The older boy shouted something angrily back.

'He thinks he's tough,' said Pete with a laugh.

'Who cares?' said John as they rode on.

He could have asked the same question all through the school day – *who cares?*

Not John. He didn't care if the teachers got angry because he was drawing and writing jokes and stories in class instead of paying attention. He didn't care when he was sent to the head teacher's office yet again.

The head teacher, Mr Pobjoy, looked at John coldly. John Lennon was not the kind of student he liked to have in his school. 'You'll be lucky if you get a job in the docks,' he told John. 'You're going *nowhere* – nowhere here at school and nowhere in life generally.'

John knew what Mr Pobjoy wanted. He was hoping that John would apologise and say that he'd try harder. That wasn't John's style. Instead, he looked the head teacher right in the eye. 'Is *nowhere* full of geniuses, sir? Because if it is, I probably belong there.'

That evening Mimi sat alone in the sitting room, a cigarette in one hand and a book in the other. The sound of Tchaikovsky on the radio filled the room. Laughter came from the stairs as John and George joked together. Mimi didn't join them; she didn't even look up from her book.

They were putting a speaker up on the wall in John's room so that he could hear the radio from downstairs in his own bedroom. Finally, John pressed the button upstairs and the sound of Tchaikovsky filled his room.

'Mimi! It works!' John ran to the top of the stairs. 'Can we see if something else is on?' He wanted some music to match his excitement, not more of Mimi's classical music.

His aunt's answer came up from the sitting room: she sounded as if she was explaining something very obvious to a little child. 'No, John. We do *not* turn Tchaikovsky over.'

Another rule of the house, but John was too excited to care. As he ran back to his room, he didn't notice how tired his uncle was looking.

Later that evening George was still in John's bedroom. John was lying on the bed, feet up on the wall. He loved having the radio speaker in his room. He and his uncle were both laughing as they listened to a comedy programme, one of his favourites.

George had poured himself a drink from a small bottle. John reached for the glass.

'You'll get me in trouble,' said George.

John smiled. 'You're always in trouble.'

'What, with Mimi? Don't be silly.'

John shook his head. He was still smiling, but he wasn't joking now. 'She never looks happy,' he said.

'Well, she's married to me!' George joked. He stood up. 'Your programme's on, and the pub's waiting for me.'

He took a step to the door, but he didn't reach it. The next moment, he fell forwards onto the floor.

John started laughing again – his uncle could never be serious for long. But then he realised that George wasn't moving. This wasn't another of his little jokes; it was real.

John could hear the note of fear in his voice as he said, 'Uncle George?'

* * *

Time stood still. Then everything seemed to happen slowly, at a distance. John didn't move. There was Mimi running to the phone, then the sound of the ambulance as it broke the silence of their quiet street.

John felt helpless. He could only stand and watch as his uncle was carried into the ambulance.

Several neighbours had come out to see what was going on. Mimi was doing the buttons on her coat and checking her hat. 'He's just had a fall,' she told them. 'There's nothing to see, really. He'll be fine.'

John wasn't so sure. He looked into the back of the ambulance and saw his uncle lift one thumb weakly. He was trying to say that he was OK.

'You stay here,' Mimi told John as she got into the ambulance. 'We'll be back soon enough.'

John watched the ambulance drive off and then he was on his own. He didn't even think about going up to his bedroom … . After several long hours of nervous waiting, he fell asleep on the sofa.

It was the middle of the night when the sound of the front door woke him. Mimi had returned from the hospital alone.

'Mimi?'

When she turned, John saw that her eyes were red. She had been crying. Mimi never cried. 'He's dead,' she said simply.

John gave a strange laugh. He couldn't stop himself. She was joking, wasn't she? She *had* to be.

Mimi walked past him into the kitchen and began to wash up. Then it hit John – it was true. His uncle was dead.

He went to put his arms around Mimi. Hot tears were in his eyes.

Mimi patted his head quickly. 'Please, let's not be silly,' she said. 'If you want to cry, go to your room.' She turned back to the washing up. 'It's just the two of us now, so let's get on with it.'

John did want to cry; he wanted Mimi to hold him. Instead, he stood next to her in silence and began to dry the dishes.

* * *

It was the first funeral John had ever been to. He felt uncomfortable in his black suit and tie. As she stood at the grave, Mimi kept her head high and held back the tears.

For John it was hard to believe that they were putting his uncle's body into the ground.

He looked around. A short distance behind them, a woman with red hair was watching the funeral. Her eyes met John's and she smiled sadly.

John watched as she turned and slowly walked away. He had recognised her immediately.

Later, everyone went back to the house. While all the adults were inside, John and his cousin, Stan, talked in the garden.

'Do you want to go to Blackpool tomorrow?' Stan asked. 'We could go on some rides at the fair.'

'You don't need to look after me, Stan,' said John quietly.

'I know – I'm just asking about Blackpool.' Stan paused. 'He was my uncle, too.'

'Yes, but he was *more* than just an uncle to me, wasn't he?' John was quiet for a moment, then he turned to his cousin. 'You saw her too, right?' he said. 'The woman with the red hair?'

Stan nodded.

John went on. 'Why isn't she here now?'

'She was busy, apparently. That's what Mimi said.' Stan looked at his cousin. 'Anyway, you should call her *Mum* ... the woman with the red hair.'

John didn't answer. Yes, the woman with red hair was his mother, but she hadn't been *Mum* to him for a long time ... .

* * *

John lay on his bed and thought. A memory kept coming back to him. How old had he been? Four? No more than five ... .

He was standing in the hall and there was someone outside the front door. A woman, a woman with red hair. She could see him through the thick glass. She hit her hand against the glass urgently.

'John!' she shouted. Her voice sounded sad, afraid, but John didn't know why. Suddenly, his Aunt Mimi appeared and carried him out of the hall and away, away from the woman with the red hair. Away from his mother.

CHAPTER 2
'Fun, Fun, Fun!'

John had told Mimi that he was going to Blackpool for the day with his cousin Stan. As they left, his aunt appeared at the front door. She crossed her arms and asked the usual question. 'John, have you got your glasses?'

'They're in my pocket.'

He knew this answer wouldn't be good enough for Mimi.

'And is your pocket blind?' she said.

It was useless to argue. As he put his glasses on, she continued, 'You will be careful, won't you? Be careful who you talk to.'

John smiled. 'We're only going to Blackpool, Mimi.'

As soon as they were round the corner, the glasses were back in John's pocket. Stan didn't speak for a moment. It was clear he had something on his mind.

'I found out where your mum lives,' he told John. 'You want to see her, right?'

John wasn't sure what to say. For years he'd thought about seeing his mother again. He hadn't expected to see her at the funeral. And now he wasn't sure if he was ready for this. Not yet. 'Yes, but … ,' he said uncertainly.

'We don't have to go,' Stan added.

'No, no,' John said quickly. He was still trying to get used to the idea. 'What bus do we get?'

'We don't,' answered Stan. 'We walk.'

John stopped for a moment, surprised. If they could walk to his mum's house, that meant she didn't live very far away.

Stan led the way and John followed in silence. It didn't take more than twenty minutes and there they were, standing outside a house. It was smaller than Mimi's, at one end of a quiet little street. Stan was already walking up to the front door, but John stayed near the gate. Why was he feeling so nervous? He wasn't ready for this, that was the answer. What could he say to his mother? What if she didn't want to see him? He wanted to turn and run.

But it was too late: Stan was already knocking on the door.

Moments later it opened, and there she was – the woman with red hair. Julia.

His mother.

It was obvious that this was a big surprise. Her eyes didn't move from John's face; she didn't even look at Stan. Without a word, she stepped forward, took her son into her arms and held him tight. At first, John wasn't sure what to do; but then he closed his eyes and hugged his mother back.

* * *

Inside, John and Stan sat at a little table with cups of tea in front of them. John looked around him: this house was very different from Mimi's. Julia had two daughters and there were toys and books everywhere. There was a record player in the corner and a lot of records. Mimi's house felt like a museum, John thought. This house was messy, but it was full of life and laughter.

Julia was busy in the kitchen. 'Bad news for Blackpool, good news for us!' she shouted. She came into the room with a plate of little cakes. 'We like Blackpool, though, don't we, girls? Fun, fun, fun!' Her two daughters, Julia and Jackie, laughed along with her.

Later, the girls were playing in the garden outside, and Stan was sitting at the piano. John had stayed at the little table. In one hand he held the harmonica that George had given him.

'Ooh, let's have a look,' said Julia quickly. She turned the instrument over in her hands, then lifted it to her mouth and pretended to play. 'Is it OK? You don't mind, do you?'

John just watched silently as she started to blow into the harmonica.

'It's a good one,' she said.

'Uncle George gave it to me,' said John with a sad smile, 'just before he died.'

Julia was suddenly serious. 'Everybody will miss him. He was a good man.'

She looked at her son, and then her huge smile appeared like the sun from behind a cloud.

'Blackpool!' she cried. 'Let's go to Blackpool, you and me! Come on!'

* * *

Fun, fun, fun. That's how Julia had described Blackpool, and it was true – being in Blackpool with Julia *was* fun, fun, fun.

John felt as if the bus ride had brought them to another world. The seaside town was full of the smell of fish and chips and the sounds of the sea and music from the fair rides. He walked arm-in-arm with his mum past the little shops that looked out onto the grey sea.

John still couldn't believe that this was happening. He smiled as his mother danced around and laughed. At one little shop, she put a silly hat on his head; the words on the front said, 'Kiss me quick'. Laughing, Julia covered John's face in kisses.

Like two children, they ran into the Hall of Mirrors and went from mirror to mirror. One made them look impossibly tall and thin, another bent their faces into strange shapes. They turned and looked into the last mirror. This one made them pause – it didn't change their appearance at all – but they were still looking at an unusual sight. Mother and son. Together.

Later that afternoon they were walking past a café, when Julia cried in excitement. 'Do you hear that?' She took John by the arm and pulled him into the café.

There was a jukebox* in there and it was playing a rock 'n' roll song. That's what Julia had heard outside. She went straight to the machine and looked at all the songs on it. The music was loud, and she began to dance to it. People in the café were looking at her, but she didn't care. John noticed that several of the young men in the café were watching, but Julia did not stop. She knew the words and sang along to the song, lost in the music.

She moved closer to John until her face was right next to his. 'Do you know what it means, rock 'n' roll?' she asked with a huge smile. Then she whispered the answer in his ear, 'Sex. That's what rock 'n' roll means.

* * *

* A jukebox is a machine in bars and cafés that plays records.

Back at Julia's house that evening, the party carried on. She had put the same song on the record player and now she and John were dancing and laughing in the middle of the living room. John tried to sing along, although he still didn't know all the words.

Stan sat in the corner: he had looked after Julia's daughters all day, and he looked tired and bored now. The girls were both asleep on the sofa.

Suddenly, a tall man appeared at the kitchen door. He didn't seem pleased with what he saw.

'Bobby!' Julia cried to him. She waved a hand at John. 'Look who's here! It's John!'

Bobby was his mum's boyfriend. He worked in the evenings and he was still wearing his waiter's clothes. He nodded and gave a tight little smile, 'Hello, John.'

It was clear that Bobby didn't share Julia's excitement that her son was here. He turned the record player off and bent down to see the two little girls asleep on the sofa.

Julia was excited and wanted to tell him everything about their day. 'We went to Blackpool! Stan looked after the girls!'

Bobby gave a quick smile. 'And they should be in bed,' he told Julia.

'But *John's* here!' continued Julia.

John wasn't sure what was happening, but he knew that the mood had changed. 'Yes, I'm here,' he said.

'Yes, and it's late,' said Bobby. The message was clear: he wanted John to leave.

Bobby gently shook the girls awake and began to lead them upstairs.

'Come on, John. We should go,' said Stan. 'It's getting dark.'

Julia followed the two boys to the door. 'Next time we'll

have even more fun,' she told John. She threw her arms around her son's neck and hugged him again. With her mouth close to his ear, she whispered, 'Don't tell Mimi, please! This is *our* secret.' Her voice sounded nervous now, almost afraid. She pulled away and looked into his eyes. 'Promise me.'

John nodded, and almost immediately Julia was happy and smiling again. As he and Stan walked away, she called after him, 'I love you! … You're my DREAM! Don't forget that.'

* * *

It was late when John got home, but Mimi hadn't gone to bed. She had a book in her hand, but John knew that she had been waiting for him to get home. He answered her questions about Blackpool, but he kept his promise: he didn't mention one word about Julia.

Upstairs in his room, it was impossible to sleep. He kept trying to sort through his feelings. His day in Blackpool had brought back memories of another day, years earlier.

He remembered the same grey sea, the same fair rides … . But this had not been a happy time, not at all. He remembered crying … looking at a clock on the wall and crying. He could hear his own voice, just two words again and again:

'Mummy … Daddy … Mummy … Daddy … .'

CHAPTER 3
'Are you looking for trouble?'

Now that he had found his mum, John didn't want to lose her for a second time. He went to her house right after school the next day.

It was Bobby who opened the door. His face darkened when he saw John. 'You can't just come round here like this, you know,' he began.

He fell silent when Julia appeared behind him. 'My DREAM is back!' she cried at the sight of John. His heart jumped. It didn't matter what Bobby thought; his mum wanted to be with him!

They went out to the cinema together. There in black and white on the big screen, he saw for the first time the big new star from America. Elvis Presley was his name, and he was the coolest thing ever. He had a guitar, but he wasn't playing it; instead, he was holding a microphone in one hand and singing the most exciting music John had ever heard. Rock 'n' roll. It wasn't just the music, it was everything – the hair, the clothes, the *look*. On the screen, the crowd – most of them girls – were all screaming for Elvis. He was like a god to them! And here in the cinema, the girls all around John were screaming for Elvis, too. John could hardly believe it. His mother's words from Blackpool came back to him, and he knew that she had been right about the meaning of rock 'n' roll.

From that moment in the dark of the cinema, John had a sudden realisation. He knew what he wanted to be.

* * *

John and Pete were in a record shop in the city centre. They both looked very different now: they had styled their hair to look cool like Elvis, and they were dressed like rock 'n' rollers, too. It was a school day, but John didn't care: he had more important things on his mind.

While Pete asked the shop owner a question, John quickly picked up several records and pushed them inside his jacket. Minutes later the boys were outside the shop and running towards the docks. As usual, there were lots of people here. In Liverpool, the docks were the place to be, the real heart of the city – the place where ships arrived from all around the world.

John pulled out the records he had stolen. He looked at the first. '*Jazz*,' he said angrily. If there was one kind of music John hated, it was jazz. Without another word, he threw the record into the dark water of the River Mersey.

The second record was the same – 'Jazz!' and the third.

'I've stolen the wrong music,' John said angrily.

He was getting ready to throw them all away into the river, when a man came up to him.

'Cool it!' he said. 'Music is music. It shouldn't ever be thrown in the river.'

John could see from the style of the man's clothes that he worked on the passenger ships that went to and from America.

'But it's *jazz*,' John told the man, as if that explained everything.

'Jazz is cool,' said the man.

'It's rubbish,' John replied.

'Tell that to Billie Holiday*.'

'I will,' said John. 'Where is he?'

The man looked at the two teenagers and thought for a moment. 'You're rock 'n' rollers, right? I've got a new record back on the ship. You can't even buy it in this country. I'll swap it for your jazz records.'

'Who's it by?'

'Screamin' Jay Hawkins,' the man told him.

* Billie Holiday was a famous American singer of blues and jazz. She was a woman!

'OK.'

As the man went to get the record, Pete gave John a look. 'I've never heard of Screamin' Jay Hawkins. Have you?'

'No,' said John. 'But I bet Mum has. Mum knows everyone.'

* * *

The two boys came back from the city centre to Woolton by bus. They didn't go inside the bus – there was a better way to travel. They climbed up onto to the top of the bus and rode there. They had to lie flat on the bus's roof so they didn't fall off. It was dangerous, but much more fun. John laughed all the way home.

When they reached their bus stop, they just jumped off. There was a gang of teenagers at the bus stop, most of them boys. John recognised one of the girls from school: her name was Marie.

John looked at the boys she was with. 'They forgot to lock the zoo today, did they? Do you always hang out with animals like this, Marie?'

These boys weren't like anyone at his school; they were a lot tougher. One of them pulled a knife from his pocket. He pointed it towards John.

'Are you looking for trouble?'

This kid was dangerous, but John never ran away from a fight. 'I won't get any trouble from someone like you,' he said.

The kid with the knife pushed the weapon closer.

Anger was always more powerful than fear for John. He stared right into the kid's eyes. 'Come on then, genius,' he said. 'It's not hard.' The knife was touching his chest now. 'Push.'

Suddenly the boy looked uncertain – what should he do? Marie pulled his arm away. 'Come on,' she said. 'Stop it.'

John nodded to Marie, and then to the boys. 'Always a pleasure,' he said.

As he walked away, John knew that Marie was watching him.

* * *

John had been right – Julia *had* heard of Screamin' Jay Hawkins. She put the record on.

This music wasn't like anything John had ever heard before: it was slower than most rock 'n' roll he knew, but there was something about it, a kind of wildness.

As she listened, Julia moved from side to side in time to the music, a cigarette in one hand.

'I can't believe you've got this,' she said with a wide smile.

'This guy at the docks swapped it.'

'For what?'

But Julia didn't really seem to care how John had got the record. She had a dreamy look in her eyes as she listened to the music. John was lying on the sofa and Julia joined him now. She lay back against him with her head on his chest and her eyes closed.

John was confused. He could feel his mother next to him, he could feel the music in his chest. It seemed as if everything in his life was changing.

* * *

'I will *not* allow students from this school to ignore their lessons and spend school days in the city centre,' said the head teacher Mr Pobjoy.

John and his friend Pete were standing in Pobjoy's office. Somebody had seen them around the docks and called the school.

'I'm suspending both of you from school,' continued the head teacher angrily. 'Your families will receive letters in the post. Peter Shotton, I don't want you near the school for a week.' He turned towards John. 'And you? I don't even know when I want you back,' he said.

More trouble was waiting for John when he got home. Mimi was sitting at the dining room table.

'I didn't see you there,' said John as he came into the room.

'Where did you see me then?' replied Mimi calmly. She gave him a hard, bright smile. John knew something was wrong.

'How was school?' Her voice was still calm.

'All right. They're killing us with homework, though. Tonight we've got Maths, French … and we mustn't forget that great favourite, History!'

'DON'T LIE TO ME, JOHN LENNON!' shouted Mimi suddenly. 'Where've you been, hmm? A neighbour called to tell me that you were on the roof of a bus! It seems that you choose to embarrass me again and again.' She shook her head angrily. 'Just remember everything I've done for you. Without me, you would be in a children's home*! Just remember that!'

'You never let me forget!' cried John.

Mimi was too angry for words. She picked up an apple from the table and threw it at John.

'Ow! That hurt!'

'Good!' shouted Mimi.

✳ ✳ ✳

After the argument, there was only one place John wanted to go. Julia was different, she wouldn't shout at him like that. She wouldn't care if he didn't do well in his lessons at school.

There was no answer when he knocked at the front door.

* A place where children can live if they have no parents or guardians.

He tried knocking again, harder.

'Hello? It's me.'

He was sure that he had seen his mother through the curtains of the front window, but she didn't move. She must have heard him, but she was just sitting there, alone.

So why wasn't she answering the door?

CHAPTER 4
'Be a Friend'

Mimi had been really angry – and she didn't know the worst yet: he had been suspended from school. How angry would she be if she knew *that*?

John didn't want to find out. That meant that he had an important job to do – he had to stop Pobjoy's letter from getting into Mimi's hands.

As soon as he saw the postman on their street early in the morning, he left the house. He was wearing his school uniform; it was important for Mimi to believe that his routine was the same as usual.

He was careful to reach the front gate at exactly the same moment as the postman. Instead of walking up to the front door, he handed the letters to John.

John quickly looked through them – it was there, the letter from the head teacher to his aunt. Now all he had to do was burn the letter and Mimi would never know a thing about it.

* * *

That still left John with a problem. While he was suspended, he still had to pretend to leave for school every day. So how should he fill his day?

The answer was easy. The first person he went to see was Julia. Together they went to a local café. She listened as he sang to her in his best 'Elvis' voice. Julia put her hands over her heart – he was the young king of rock 'n' roll and she was one of his screaming fans.

John sat down heavily. 'Why couldn't God make *me* Elvis?'

Julia smiled. 'He was saving you for John Lennon.'

He lifted his eyes to the sky. 'I'll get you for that, God!'

John looked at his mum. 'Do you want to go to the fair tomorrow?'

'What about school?'

John paused. He could never have told Mimi, but it was different with his mum. 'I've … been suspended.'

Julia sighed. 'Oh, John … what for?'

It was hard not to laugh as he said, 'Going into town during school hours and stealing records.'

Julia's eyes met his. 'You haven't told Mimi, have you?'

John shook his head. 'I don't want to listen to all the rubbish she'd say about it. There's no point.'

'Why? She has to listen to all *your* rubbish.'

'Well, I never asked her to, did I?' John said quietly. Julia said nothing. John knew that this was a painful subject for her; it was for him, too.

'Can I stay with you?' he continued. 'Just during the day, while I'm suspended? Mimi still thinks I'm at school.' He pulled a funny face. 'Go on,' he said. 'Be a friend.'

Julia didn't reply, but John already knew from the look in her eyes: the answer was *yes*.

* * *

'If you're here, why not learn something?' said Julia.

They were in her living room, and she was sitting opposite John with a banjo in her hands.

'You hold it like this,' she said. Slowly she moved her right hand over the strings. 'Move your hand from the wrist.'

When John laughed, she told him, 'Be serious, or I'll phone Mimi myself.' It was clear from the look on her face that she was only joking.

John put his glasses on to watch more closely. She started to sing an old song – 'Maggie May'. John could hardly believe it – she was really good.

'Wow,' he said when the song was over.

Julia just shrugged, then she passed the banjo to him – it was his turn to play. He carefully put his hands and fingers in the correct position.

'Try and hit all the strings,' Julia told him.

He wasn't much good at first, but somehow it felt right

to have an instrument in his hands like this. He moved his fingers over the strings once, then checked the position of his hands and tried again. He continued in this way for hours. He was still practising when Julia's daughters came home from school. They played, shouted and laughed, but John ignored everything except that banjo. He was still playing when Bobby came home from work later that evening.

After a few days, he was sounding good. He couldn't play anything difficult yet, but he could do a rock 'n' roll song well enough. As John played and sang a Buddy Holly* song 'That'll be the Day', Julia played the piano with him. They started off slowly at first so that he could get the chord changes right, but it was sounding good.

When he realised that Julia had stopped playing, John cried, 'Come on, Mum. You're missing it!'

A sharp voice from behind him cried, 'NO, Julia!'

It was Mimi. She was standing at the door. Julia was staring at her with fear in her eyes. Mimi waved a hand at the room. She continued to speak to Julia. 'This may be your life – one big *mess* – but it is not his.' She stepped into the room. 'I received a telephone call from the school today. Do you know that he has been SUSPENDED FROM SCHOOL?' She looked at John angrily.

'Yes,' Julia managed to say. She sounded like a frightened child with an angry parent.

Mimi turned to John. 'Come on – out!' she ordered.

John did not move.

'I *mean* it!' warned Mimi.

John looked from his mother to his aunt. He had loved these days with his mum and didn't want them to end. He

* Buddy Holly was an American rock 'n'roll singer. He was famous for his thick glasses.

gave a little shake of his head. *No.*

John's reply seemed to bring Julia back to life. She jumped up. 'Get out of my house.' She pushed Mimi towards the door. 'Go.'

As Mimi walked angrily out of the house, Julia took John in her arms. He just sat there. He had lived with Mimi and followed all her rules for years. What now? 'What have I done?' he thought to himself.

* * *

Life at Julia's house was very different. For dinner the whole family crowded round the little dining table and ate fish and chips from the chip shop with their fingers. The two little girls liked John; they laughed at every funny face and silly joke. Julia loved having John here, too. Only Bobby stayed quiet.

That night Julia brought John a glass of milk at bedtime. He looked at the room around him – it was full of his half-sister's toys.

'I've stolen little Julia's bed,' he said, embarrassed.

'She's your sister – she's happy you're here,' answered his mother.

'How long can I stay?' John asked.

Julia smiled, but there was something sad about it. Without a word, she kissed John's head and stood up.

'Night, night,' she said, as she left the room.

In his dreams, John was a small boy again, back in Blackpool.

He heard a small boy's voice – his own voice. 'Mummy … Daddy … Mummy … Daddy.'

His parents were there and they were arguing, but John didn't know why.

He remembered something else – Aunt Mimi had been there, too. She wasn't with his mum and dad, she was waiting in a café outside.

But why? How did all these memories fit together? What had happened in Blackpool all those years ago?

John opened his eyes. It took him a moment to remember where he was. He could hear voices downstairs – Bobby and Julia. John went to the top of the stairs to hear them better.

'I'll get a job,' Julia was saying.

'And who's going to look after the girls?' said Bobby.

'I'll work part-time,' added Julia, 'at the café – anywhere. I can do this!'

Bobby raised his voice. 'No, you *can't*! It'll all be too much for you … again.'

John held his breath and listened. What did he mean *again*?

Bobby continued, 'I'll lose you again, and I need you. The girls need you.'

'Yes, and I need John!' said Julia urgently. 'I am his mother.'

'Mimi's been looking after him since he was five years old.'

'I never wanted that!' Julia was crying now. 'Bobby, it's not fair!'

'But that's how it turned out,' he said. 'Mimi needs John.'

'I need him! I need him to be mine!'

Bobby's voice became softer. 'He'll be all right. Listen to me – *for the girls*, we can't lose you again. He's got to go … , OK?'

Unseen on the stairs, John listened as his mother finally answered.

'OK.'

* * *

The next morning, John was wearing his school uniform when he came downstairs.

Bobby and the girls were having breakfast at the little table, while Julia washed dishes in the kitchen.

'I … think I'll just go,' said John. 'It's wrong taking little Julia's bed.'

His mother became very still. She didn't turn around.

'Thanks for the banjo lessons,' said John. Julia still said nothing; she didn't move. 'Mum? Mum … .'

John could see the tears on her face in the little kitchen mirror on the wall.

He turned and left the house.

* * *

Mimi was sitting at the breakfast table, still in her night clothes. When she saw John at the door, she said quietly, 'Have you decided where you're living now?'

John didn't speak. He just took his jacket off and joined her at the table. Something had changed between them; what was it? Mimi didn't seem angry now, she wasn't shouting at him. She sounded sad as she said, 'She'll hurt you. You know that, don't you?'

She reached across the table, patted his head.

John lifted his eyes. He had made an important decision. 'I'm going to start a rock 'n' roll group,' he told her.

CHAPTER 5
'That's rock 'n' roll'

John and Mimi took the bus into the city centre. We must look strange together, John thought. He was wearing his leather jacket and blue jeans – all very rock 'n' roll – but he had his glasses on, too. Mimi was dressed smartly as usual, but her dark, old-fashioned clothes made her look older than she was.

They were going to a music shop. For John it was a place of dreams, full of guitars and other musical instruments. He chose one guitar and sat down to try it.

'It's just three chords,' he told Mimi as he played. 'That's rock 'n' roll. It's simple!'

'You have to be simple to like it,' replied Mimi coolly.

'Funny,' said John. 'Well done.'

Mimi pretended to hit him. 'It's not exactly Bach though, is it?'

The shop owner joined them and nodded at the guitar in John's hands. 'That's a nice little instrument. It plays well, and I can give you a very good price.'

'What's very good about it?' asked Mimi. John smiled to himself. He could hear the strength in his aunt's voice.

'Eight pounds,' said the shop owner.

'That's not very good,' she replied immediately. 'Is it, John?'

'Not very good at all,' John said. 'Very good would be … '

'Seven pounds,' finished Mimi. 'Cash.'

'*That's* very good,' John agreed.

They both stared at the shop owner. He didn't have a chance against Mimi and John Lennon together and he knew it.

'OK, seven pounds, cash,' he sighed.

When they got home, John went straight to his room. He placed his new guitar on his bed against the wall and stared at it. This was better! Elvis Presley didn't play the banjo; rock 'n' roll was all about guitars! As John looked at his guitar, he imagined that he was looking into his future. Now he had to go out and make it happen.

* * *

Back in school, John called a meeting of his friends. He was the leader of the group and everyone knew it: when John Lennon called you for a meeting, you went.

'What's up, John?'

John smiled. 'You've been chosen to be in my band.'

The other boys began to laugh; John must be joking, as usual. But their laughter died. They realised that he was serious.

'A band, John? But I don't know how to play anything.'

'Me neither!'

John shook his head. Little problems like that weren't

going to get in his way. 'It's a skiffle* band!' he told them. 'You don't have to *know* how to play! What's important is this: I've chosen you, and we're going to be great.'

'What if we're rubbish?' asked Pete.

John had an answer ready. 'Shut up!' He turned to another boy. 'Eric, you've got a guitar, right? And Rod, you said that you've got a banjo.'

'Yeah. '

'OK,' continued John. Nobody was going to say *no* to him and he knew it. 'First practice is on Thursday at Pete's house. You'd better not be late! Questions?'

'Have we got a name?' asked Rod.

John patted his friend on the cheek. 'Yes, Rodders, we have!'

And that was the end of the meeting.

* * *

John wasn't going to show it, but he was feeling nervous. The day of the Woolton village fair had arrived, and the sun was shining. Everything looked the same as it did every year: there were children's games and tents with tea and cakes. Proud gardeners stood next to tables of their best vegetables. In the main area, a small crowd was watching a show by a policeman and his dog.

There was just one difference: today John and his band were playing their first concert. Their name was The Quarrymen – John's idea, of course. He had taken the name from their school, Quarry Bank.

The band waited nervously behind a lorry. John checked his hair one last time in the side mirror.

* Skiffle was a kind of music popular in the UK in the 1950s, before rock 'n' roll. It was often played with unusual instruments, including things from around the house.

'Right. Are we ready to do this, boys?' No answer. 'I said ARE WE READY TO DO THIS?'

'Yes.'

'Yeah, John.'

John nodded. Even if you didn't feel confident, it was important to *look* confident. 'Then let's do it.'

The band climbed onto the back of the flat lorry, which was their stage today, and John took the microphone.

A small crowd began to form.

'Go, Johnny boy!' shouted a voice John knew well – it was Julia, here with her two daughters.

John pretended that he couldn't see her. 'Where've you gone?' Their eyes met. 'I've lost you … .' He smiled as he turned to the rest of the small crowd. 'Oh, there you all are!'

The band began to play 'Maggie May', the first song that Julia had taught him on her banjo. Near the front of the crowd, she was singing along to the words while her two little girls danced. Mimi was there too, but she stood at the back of the crowd.

John knew that the Quarrymen weren't the most skilful band in the world: some of them weren't much more than beginners on their instruments. But he also knew that the crowd liked them. All eyes were on him, and he liked it. His voice was strong, with just a little roughness at the edges. As he stood at the front of the band, a powerful feeling hit him: this was his place, he *belonged* here.

* * *

After the concert, the band went to the church hall and had a drink to celebrate. John was feeling good about their performance: he had done it, he had actually stood on stage and sung.

He didn't look up at first when a kid called Ivan came in and said, 'Hey everyone, this is my friend from school, Paul.'

The boy called Paul was a tall, thin kid. He looked younger than John, and he was wearing a white jacket with a flower pinned to it.

'Paul plays, too,' continued Ivan.

'What, with toys?' joked John. He turned and saw that the new kid had a guitar over his shoulder.

John held his hand out. 'I'm John.'

The new kid introduced himself. 'Paul.'

'Want a beer?'

'I'd love a tea.'

A *tea!* John turned to the guys in the band. 'Is there any tea left?' he asked, jokingly.

His eyes returned to Paul. 'So? Did you watch us play?'

'Yeah,' said Paul.

'And?'

'Yeah, you're all right.'

All right? That wasn't good enough. John took a step closer. Who did this kid think he was? 'We're *all right*?' His eyes did not move from Paul's face. Then suddenly he smiled and patted Paul's arm. 'You're all right … . Ivan likes you, and he's all right.' He nodded at Paul's guitar. 'How all right are you on one of those?'

In answer, Paul moved the guitar round and got ready to play.

John noticed he was going to play with his left hand. 'You've got that back-to-front, haven't you?' he said. The rest of the band laughed.

They stopped laughing as Paul began to play. He was good – really good – and he could sing, too. His voice was higher than John's, less rough, but the whole performance was great rock 'n' roll.

The guys in the band knew he was good. John knew it, too, but he wasn't going to say that. He was used to being number one. 'How old are you?' he asked, when Paul had finished playing.

'Fifteen, last month.' Paul looked back down at his guitar. 'I can do Little Richard* songs, too.'

'Sorry, no time,' John interrupted. 'We've got another concert to play today.' The message was clear: *go away.*

'Oh.' Paul seemed a bit surprised. 'Well, I'd better go anyway,' he said.

'OK, bye.' *Just go away.*

As Paul and Ivan turned to leave, one of the band said quietly to John, 'I'd rather have him in our band than in someone else's.'

John knew that was true. He turned and called to the new kid, 'What's your name again?'

The boy stopped at the door. 'Paul,' he answered. 'Paul McCartney.'

* Little Richard was an American rock 'n' roll singer who played the piano.

CHAPTER 6
'It's the music – simple'

Mimi looked out of the window when she heard someone at the front door.

'John, your little friend's here,' she shouted up the stairs.

This was John's new routine: Paul came round with his guitar and the two practised together.

Paul was a better musician, and he patiently showed John the chords. John paused and put on his new glasses so that he could see the exact position of Paul's fingers on the guitar strings. He saw the look of surprise on Paul's face and the start of a smile.

'It's my Buddy Holly look,' John joked.

Paul just nodded. 'Good,' he said, and he continued to play the guitar.

The two played for hours. After one practice, John

asked, 'So it's cool with Mummy that baby Paul wants to be Elvis?' He wondered for a moment what kind of mother Paul had. Was she like Mimi? Or Julia?

'She would have loved it,' said Paul.

'Rubbish!'

'No, she's not around any more.'

John paused. 'What?'

'She … died,' said Paul. 'Last year.'

John didn't know what to say. Paul changed the subject. 'You know, if we're going to do this, we should write our own stuff. That way the record companies don't get all the money.'

'I write stuff,' said John. 'More poems and little stories than songs … .' He was thinking of the things he wrote during lessons at school when he ought to be paying attention.

'Write a tune for them and you've got a song,' said Paul. It sounded so simple.

'Have you written any songs?' John asked him.

Paul shrugged. 'A couple.'

John was learning that there was a lot more to Paul than he'd thought at first. 'Why do you know so much?' he asked. 'I mean, you don't seem like a very rock 'n' roll guy.'

'Why's that? Because I don't go around making trouble and getting into fights?'

'Yeah,' said John.

Paul gave another shrug. 'It's the music – simple,' he said.

* * *

Paul's advice stuck in his head. John continued to practise the guitar every day, but he also began to write more. He still produced his funny stories and strange little pictures. But he began to try and write music, as well. Maybe Paul was right: maybe it *was* simple.

But then one day after school, he got a surprise. He saw that his guitar wasn't in its usual place on his bed. It wasn't under the bed either, or in the wardrobe. Strange … .

John ran downstairs. Mimi was sitting at the table, eating a bowl of soup.

'Where is it?' John asked her.

Mimi carefully put down her spoon.

'Where's my guitar?'

'Your school report arrived today,' said Mimi coldly. 'You promised me hard work. You can lie to others as much as you like. If you lie to me, there will be a PRICE TO PAY!' She picked up the report and threw it towards him.

John ignored it. He didn't care about the report; there was just one thing on his mind, the guitar. 'Where IS it?'

'I've sold it.'

John couldn't believe this. 'You *can't*!'

'I can and I have.'

'But we've got concerts!' cried John.

'Oh, what a pity! *Grow* up, John. Stop behaving like a child.'

The anger had been growing inside John. Now it exploded.

'Shut up, Mimi!'

'*What* did you say to me?'

'SHUT UP!'

He turned and ran wildly to the door and out of the house. Twenty minutes later he was in the music shop. So it was true, she really had sold his guitar. There it was on the wall. The shop was selling it for five pounds now.

Mimi didn't understand how important this was to him. But John knew somebody who *would* understand. He ran to Julia's house as fast as he could. She was surprised to see him, but there was no time for explanations.

'Can I have five pounds?' he asked his mother urgently. Julia looked at him for a moment and then she got out her purse.

John took the money without a *thank you*, and ran off to get the guitar.

When he came home that night, Mimi was sitting with a book. John held up the guitar proudly. His smile was hard. 'So … I got it back,' he told his aunt.

Mimi said nothing, so John went further. 'Yeah, *Mum* bought it for me.'

★ ★ ★

The days of concerts at little village fairs were in the past for the Quarrymen now. The band were sounding much better, and they looked better, too; they all played in smart white jackets now. People had begun to talk about them, and a growing number of fans in the area came to concerts.

Julia was always there in the crowd, usually somewhere near the front. She loved to see John on stage, to hear him sing. She knew all the words and she liked to sing along.

John felt as if his dream was coming true, but not everything was perfect. He had started to realise that he wasn't the only star of the band now. There was Paul, too.

After one song on stage, John nodded to the crowd. 'Thanks, guys.'

At almost the same moment, Paul spoke into his microphone: 'Thank you.' John gave him a quick sideways look. This was *his* band; why was *Paul* thanking the audience?

But it was impossible to keep Paul down.

'Next Liverpool's answer to Duane Eddy* will play,' John told the crowd. 'I present to you … Mr Paul McCharmley!'

If Paul was annoyed that John had made a joke with his name, he didn't show it. 'Thanks, John,' he said into his microphone. 'Kind words.'

'I didn't mean them,' John fired back. Several people in the crowd laughed, with Julia the loudest of all.

But then Paul began to play. The rest of the band joined in, but all eyes were on Paul. People in the audience started dancing.

As he played, John looked out into the audience. Julia was dancing, too. John noticed that for once she wasn't looking at him; like everyone in the hall, all her attention was on Paul.

* * *

After the concert, the band rode home upstairs on the night bus.

Paul had asked a friend of his to come to the concert, and this friend was still with them. He sat on the bus with his guitar across his knees.

'This is George,' Paul told the others. 'He should be in the group.'

John looked at the quiet dark-haired kid in the leather jacket. He looked even younger than Paul. 'You should be in bed,' John told him.

'I've been to bed,' George answered. 'I couldn't sleep.'

'Go on, George,' Paul suggested. 'Show them.'

John watched, careful not to show too much interest, as George picked up the guitar. He changed his mind as soon as George began to play. John had to admit he was good. *Very* good.

* Duane Eddy was an American rock 'n'roll guitarist.

Before he had finished the song, John had decided: George Harrison had to be in the band.

This meant that the band had six members now. With another guitarist, their sound was fuller, bigger. They were becoming more and more popular in the area. When he was on stage, John felt alive. He loved the idea of all those people in the crowd looking up at him – all those *girls* in the crowd looking up at him … . At the end of each concert, the cheers from the crowd seemed to be louder than before.

After one concert, the party continued in the rooms behind the stage. Lots of people were there and they all wanted to be near the band. With a beer in his hand, John enjoyed being the centre of it all. There was just one problem – Julia. His mother was always around. She came to almost every concert; she was there after every concert, too.

John could see her now at the party. She was telling Paul how great the concert had been. Paul was nodding politely – Paul always seemed to be polite and friendly. But it was clear he wasn't really interested.

'We need to celebrate!' cried Julia to the whole band. Her voice was just a little too loud, her smile was a little too bright and nervous. 'It's John's birthday soon. Let's have a party at my house. This Saturday, OK?'

'Can we drink beer?' asked Pete.

'Only if I can,' said Julia.

'What do you think, John?' one of the band asked.

'I think … ,' John paused. He knew that all eyes were on him. He knew that Julia was waiting for him to say *yes* to the party. 'I need to use the toilet!'

There was the sound of laughter as he turned and walked away.

It was Paul who stopped him later. 'If you don't want

her hanging out with the band all the time, do something about it,' he said.

As Paul walked away, John just stood there. 'It's *my* group,' he said to himself angrily.

CHAPTER 7
'Where's Daddy, Mummy?'

On the night of the party, Julia's house was full of teenagers – dancing, talking and drinking.

The party was all for John, but he wasn't in the mood to celebrate. When he arrived, Bobby was at the door in his best suit. John didn't even look at him. He went straight in and got himself a drink.

He found his mother in the kitchen. She was listening to Paul as he played his guitar and sang a slow Elvis song. An anger that he couldn't explain burned inside John at the sight of it.

When the song finished, Julia patted Paul on the leg. 'That was for her, wasn't it? Your mum?' She shook her head sadly. 'It's terrible that she was taken away from you like that. It's not fair.'

She hadn't seen John at the door until he spoke. 'She got ill and died. What's your excuse?'

Julia's smile disappeared. Without a word or another look at her son, she stood up and left the kitchen.

Paul met John's eyes. 'Nice,' he said.

John gave him a hard smile.

In the main room someone had turned the rock 'n' roll record off. They had put another song on the record player. It was old, from the 1930s probably, and it wasn't very popular with the kids at the party. Then John heard the song's title and he understood. It was called 'Oh John, my Son, to Me You Are so Wonderful.' Only one person could have put this record on: Julia must have chosen it for him.

She came into the room now with a birthday cake with seventeen lit candles on top. Everybody cheered. Julia had

a big smile on her face as she brought the cake to John, but
there was a nervousness behind her eyes.

She held the cake up for him to blow out the candles.
He did this and then said loudly, 'Now could someone
turn this record off before I start crying – *in pain*!'

John knew that his words were hurting Julia, but
tonight he didn't care. Bobby was staring at him angrily,
but John didn't care about that either.

'How about a few words, John?' someone shouted.

The room became silent. 'Thanks for coming,
everybody,' John began. 'You're all very special to me … .'
Then he put on a silly voice. ' … because I *hate* you all!'

Laughter from the room.

'Except you, Mum,' John turned to Julia. 'Obviously … .
Thanks for all this … . Well everyone? What about a cheer
for Julia? Come on!'

When the room was quiet again, John continued. 'And
my band … what can I say? You're always there for me
… usually late … and you always look like rubbish, but

you're there … or somewhere not far away.' He put on an American accent. 'So where are we going, boys?'

'To the top of the top, Johnny!' Paul and the other Quarrymen shouted back.

There was more laughter. Then John saw that Julia had her arm around Paul. He felt the old anger return.

Someone put the music back on and the party continued. But John wasn't in the mood for dancing. He stood alone and drank. He watched his mother from across the room. She was sitting on Bobby's knee at the piano now and kissing him.

After a few minutes, she went outside to have a cigarette. John followed her. He found her on the low wall around the front garden. When she saw him, she jumped up. She seemed nervous, as if she didn't know what to expect from him tonight.

Julia nodded up at the black sky. 'I wonder if someone on Mars is having a quick cigarette like me,' she said.

John ignored this. 'Where's Dad?' he said. When Julia didn't answer, he went on. 'They're called *dads*, aren't they? Most people I know have got one.'

'I don't think –' Julia began, but John interrupted her:

'Don't you, Mum? Well, I do. *Think, think, think.* That's all I do … . Where's Daddy, Mummy?'

Julia turned away, tears in her eyes.

'Alf,' John went on. 'That's his name, yeah?' Julia managed a nod. 'Where's Alf then? WHERE?'

'Please don't shout, John!'

'Oh, it makes you feel uncomfortable, does it? Well, try being me for the last seventeen years, when everyone asks why you auntie's your mum. Now *that's* uncomfortable.'

Julia put one hand to her head. Tears fell down her face.

The sight of them did nothing to soften John. 'Oh, here we go,' he said. 'Who turned the water taps on?'

'Please don't be horrible to me, John,' Julia said through her tears.

'Oh, I see. Horrible John, naughty John … *poor* Julia.'

She tried to leave, but John pulled her back. 'I know you're good at running away, but you're not running away tonight. WHERE IS HE?'

'New Zealand!' Julia cried. 'Maybe … .'

'Not round the corner like you?' said John.

Julia sounded calmer, ready to tell the truth. 'He was in the Merchant Navy*,' she said. 'He left us with nothing. No letters, no money.'

'Then *you* left *me!*' cried John.

'It wasn't supposed to be for long … Mimi agreed.'

'Not for long!' John cried in disbelief. 'I'm *still* living with her!'

'I wanted you back!' cried Julia. 'I always wanted you back!'

'Oh, I believe you!' said John. '*Honest.*'

'She never gave you back!'

'But you're my mum,' John said simply.

Julia reached out for her son. She tried to explain. 'Mimi loves you so much.'

'Yeah.' John pulled away. 'More than you.'

'Mummy?' said a little girl's voice from the house. Julia's daughter had come outside. 'Mummy … I'm tired now.' The little girl looked at the tears on her mother's face. 'Are you sad again?' she asked.

'Mummy's not sad,' said Julia. 'Look!' She turned on a big – and completely false – smile. 'You go back inside. I'm coming in.'

* Ships which carry things to and from the country by sea.

When the girl had gone, Julia put her arms around John. 'I do love you … believe me.'

John stood completely still. 'Believe me, I'd love to.'

He walked off into the night.

'Where are you going?' Julia called after him.

'Away from you,' he said over his shoulder.

* * *

It was late when he arrived back at Mimi's house.

Everything was quiet. Mimi was still at the dinner table. In front of her, the table was covered with plates of food; Mimi had made him a special birthday dinner. It was all cold now.

Mimi smiled and tried not to show her disappointment. 'You said you'd be back.'

John looked at the cake with its unlit candles in the middle of the table.

'It was meant to be a surprise,' Mimi said. She seemed embarrassed – she had tried to do something nice for him, and it had gone wrong. She looked towards the corner of the room.

John couldn't believe his eyes when he saw it. It was a new electric guitar! A birthday card had been taped to it. Mimi had bought him exactly what he wanted!

'Mimi … .' He went to hug her, but she pushed him away.

'You smell of beer!'

'Mum gave a party for me,' John explained.

As soon as he said this, the mood changed.

'Oh,' said Mimi. She looked down at the cake on the table. 'This is a waste then.' She picked it up and began to carry it through to the kitchen.

There was a knock at the front door.

'Tell your friends the party's over!' shouted Mimi from the kitchen.

But it wasn't one of John's friends at the door – it was Julia.

At first John just looked at her and said, 'No thanks.' As if she was a stranger, as if she was trying to sell something they didn't want. He closed the door before she could say a word.

He changed his mind almost immediately. That wasn't enough, he was too angry. He opened the door again and roughly pulled Julia inside.

'We've got a guest!' he shouted to Mimi.

There was fear in Julia's voice now. 'I need to talk to John!'

'Oh, more talking?' said John. 'Wow!'

Mimi appeared at the kitchen door and looked coldly at her younger sister.

'You see, Mum and I have been talking,' John said to his aunt. 'Yes, she told me things about … oh, what's his name? Alf!' His words came out quickly, along with all the anger and hurt inside him. 'Oh yes, and she told me things about you, Mimi. Yes, she said you *stole* me. What do you think, Mimi? Did you steal me?'

'I never said that!' interrupted Julia.

John was becoming more and more upset. 'You said she never gave me back. Now, when *I* don't give things back, it's usually because I'm *stealing*!'

Mimi stared hard at Julia. 'Did she mention why I stole you?' she asked.

'There she is,' John answered. 'Ask her yourself.'

CHAPTER 8
'I'm going out of my mind'

Julia looked frightened, but Mimi was too angry to stop now. 'Did she mention having another man's child?' she asked John. 'Another daughter?'

'Mimi, please … ,' said Julia weakly.

'Please what?' cried Mimi. 'Look at him! Do you think we can stop now?'

John was confused, hurt. He looked at his mother. 'Whose child?' he managed to say. 'What daughter?'

Julia did not answer; she couldn't. She couldn't even meet John's eyes.

It was Mimi who said, 'Your mother has always needed *company*. Do you understand what I mean by company?'

John nodded and looked at his mother. 'Rock 'n' roll, eh, Mum?'

Mimi continued. 'And she found it, with a young man while your father was away at sea during the war*. You have another sister – Victoria.'

This was all so hard to believe. 'Where is she?' John asked.

'We don't know,' replied Mimi. 'Your mother gave her away and a home was found for her … .'

John felt suddenly weak. He sat down on the sofa. He couldn't look at either of them. Mimi hadn't finished. 'Then not long after that, your mother found another man – Bobby. She was still married to your father, but that didn't matter to her. And she was going to bring you up like that. As if that was all right! As if that was *normal*!'

John looked up at Julia who stood silent and helpless as her older sister spoke.

* Alf Lennon was away during World War II.

'When your father came home after the war, he wanted to try and save the marriage. She wasn't interested! She told him to *go away*! But Alf didn't give up that easily, did he?' Mimi came close to her sister. 'Did he, Julia? Hmm? Please join the conversation any time you like.'

Julia wasn't able to speak.

'No, I didn't think so,' said Mimi. She went to the sofa and sat by John. She patted his leg. 'You were staying here with me when Alf turned up. He said he wanted to take you to Liverpool for the day. I thought he was telling the truth, but he took you to Blackpool instead. He *kidnapped* you. He'd got himself a job in New Zealand and he was planning to take you there with him by ship. We had no idea where you were. Luckily, we got the name of one of Alf's relatives in Blackpool, and your mother and I went there to find you. When we arrived, Alf wouldn't let me inside the house. He said this was between him and your mother.'

As John listened to his aunt, all the half-memories of that time in Blackpool fitted into place in his mind. Just five years old, he had sat on the sofa and watched as his mum and dad argued. His dad asked for another chance; he wanted to make the marriage work, to keep the family together.

'It was no use,' Mimi said. She turned to John. 'But that left a problem. What to do with you? And so they had a *brilliant* idea. They decided to ask you – a five-year-old boy – who you wanted to live with for the rest of your life!'

John remembered, he remembered everything about that terrible day in Blackpool. He had looked from his mum to his dad. He said their names again and again. 'Mummy … Daddy … Mummy … Daddy … .'

His dad became impatient. 'Who do you want to be with, John? Do you want to be with me or do you want to be with your mum?'

John remembered his answer, all those years ago, just one word – 'Daddy.'

Without another word, Julia had turned around and walked out of the house. The little boy ran after her, but Julia just carried on walking.

'She knew that Alf was planning to take you to New Zealand,' explained Mimi. 'She knew that she would probably never see you again. Your mother knew all that and still she walked out. And that is when I STOLE you.' Mimi was shouting now. 'And if that's stealing, then I'm a thief!'

John's memories began to fall into place. Mimi had brought him back to her house to live with her and Uncle George. Julia had come to get him – that's when she had knocked on the glass of the front door and cried 'John!'

John was back on his feet. It was all too much for him – all those years of secrets and lies, anger and hurt.

'I had no choice!' continued Mimi.

'Oh, you had a choice!' Julia had suddenly found her voice. 'You chose to take my son.' She walked across the room to John. 'I was never going to leave you.'

'You walked out the door!' he cried. 'You walked down the street!'

'Yes, yes, I did but I was ill.' Julia was speaking quickly now. She sounded afraid. 'I get ill. I can't think properly, I can't sleep! I've seen doctors but they can't help … .'

John was pulling away towards the hall.

Julia tried to hold him back. '*I* don't understand,' she cried, 'but I'm here now, I'm *here*. I never meant to leave you … . Please. I love you, John. I love you. I'm sorry, I'm sorry … .' She tried to take him in her arms.

'No,' cried John. He pushed her away. 'I said NO!'

Julia fell to the floor and John stood and looked down at

her. This was tearing him to pieces.

'Can't you see what you're doing to me?' he cried wildly. 'I'm going out of my mind. And that's not fair!' He took a breath. 'IS it? This is your fault!' He looked up at Mimi, who was watching from the door of the living room. 'And yours! So why should *I* go mad? I've had enough. It's over!' As he left the house, he shut the door loudly behind him.

Outside he started to walk away, out into the cool darkness of the night. Away from Mimi, away from Julia … away from everything. He began to run.

He wandered on. He didn't care about where he was going. Eventually he found himself in the centre of Liverpool. It was late, but there were still a lot of people out on Matthew Street. There was a long queue to get into The Cavern*. John saw that a rock 'n' roll band called Rory Storm and the Hurricanes** was playing there.

He walked right to the front of the queue. Two big men in black suits were guarding the door. They took one look at John and said, 'No chance.'

Any other time, John might have argued; he might have been ready to fight. Tonight he just walked away.

* * *

John woke up to the grey light of early morning. He could hear water, birds – all the sounds of the River Mersey. He had slept on a seat on the pavement near the docks.

---

* The Cavern was the Liverpool club where the Beatles played their most famous early concerts.

** This was the Liverpool band Ringo Starr played in before the Beatles.

He got up slowly. His body hurt all over. There were cuts on the back of one of his hands … . Had he been in a fight last night? He couldn't remember.

There was a glass on the ground with a little beer still in it. John picked it up and walked closer to the water's edge. He looked out on Liverpool. His city. A passenger boat was moving slowly across the river.

John finished the last of the drink and turned to go home – home to Mimi's house.

★ ★ ★

In his own room again, John lay on his bed and thought. He heard the sound of the front door and pulled back the curtain to look outside. It was still quite early but Mimi was going somewhere. She was wearing a black coat and she had a scarf around her head. She was carrying some flowers from the back garden. John knew where she was going … .

He got dressed quickly and left the house. When he found her, Mimi was still arranging the flowers on Uncle George's grave. She didn't see him until he spoke.

'Did you love him?'

Mimi jumped. 'You frightened me to death.'

John looked around. 'This is the right place for it.' His voice became softer as he asked again. 'Did you?'

'That's a horrible thing to say,' answered Mimi.

'You never showed it.'

'Or you just didn't see it.'

John thought that over. 'With *my* eyes, possibly.' He paused for a moment. 'I'm not going to keep on hating her for it … for what she did in Blackpool.'

'Forgive and forget, I suppose,' said Mimi. She didn't look up.

'Forget? I wish … . There's just no point hating someone you love. I mean *really* love.' He bent down so that he was looking right at his aunt. 'Is there, Mimi?'

She kept on arranging the flowers.

John stood. 'I should move out of the house.'

'What?' Mimi sounded surprised.

'It's time,' said John. 'And who knows? If I'm gone, maybe you and Mum will remember that you were sisters once.'

He kissed his fingers and rested them on top of George's grave. As he walked away, part of him felt as if he was saying goodbye to something forever.

* * *

Mimi had looked at the phone for a long time before she called her sister. When she did call, it was surprisingly easy. They arranged to meet in a local café.

Julia was already there when Mimi arrived.

'It's good to see you,' said Julia quietly. They were both looking for the right words. They hadn't spoken to each other properly for years.

'I am not here to say I was wrong, Julia,' began Mimi. 'Not about John. I want that to be clear, but … .' Her eyes were wet with tears. This wasn't easy for her to say. '… perhaps I haven't always been right.'

Julia looked at her older sister. If she tried to speak, she would start to cry. Mimi reached for her hand. 'I do love you,' she said simply. 'I hope you know that.'

CHAPTER 9
'She's never coming back'

Months had passed since the night of John's birthday party, and life had changed. He wasn't at school any more; he was a student at Liverpool Art College now.

As he went home, John carried some college work under his arm and his guitar over his shoulder. He was feeling good, confident about the future – school was behind him and it felt as if his doubtful years were behind him, too. He knew where he was heading now.

At Mimi's house, he saw a sight that made him stop. Months earlier, it would have been impossible. Both Mimi and Julia were sitting in the back garden with cups of tea. They both had their faces turned up to the autumn sun, although it was cold enough to keep their coats on. They looked happy – two sisters enjoying the weather and each other's company in silence.

For a long moment John just enjoyed the sight of them

together. Then he walked over to join them.

'Hello young ladies,' he said.

Mimi and Julia both smiled up at him.

'It's a nice day,' John said.

Julia took off her sunglasses. 'Everything feels so different when the sun shines.'

'Usually warmer,' said John.

'How was college?' Mimi asked him.

'All right. We painted a woman with no clothes on. She was the one with no clothes on, you understand, not us … .'

Mimi tried to hide her smile, while Julia laughed.

John turned to leave.

'Where are you going?' asked Mimi. She was hoping that he would stay for a while.

'Paul's waiting for me at his house. I just needed to leave my art stuff here.'

'What about dinner?' Mimi continued.

'I'm not hungry.'

'Well, you will be.'

'He could have his dinner at my house,' suggested Julia. She gave Mimi a quick look and added, 'You know, because Paul's house is near mine … . If you're not making anything special … maybe?'

With her eyes closed again, Mimi thought this over. 'It saves me from cooking, I suppose.'

John and Julia shared a secret smile.

'Oh, go on,' said Julia. 'Sit down with us for a while.'

She didn't need to persuade him too much. With a smile, he sat down with his mum and his aunt.

* * *

At Paul's house, John turned the tape recorder on and began to play his guitar. Paul sat opposite him and listened carefully. The song was a new one. It was called 'Hello, Little Girl' and it was the first song that John had ever written.

He felt good about it. He was proud of the song, and singing it felt somehow different. Better. This was something that was completely *his*. And Paul had liked the song, too. Life was looking good. Then the phone rang.

Mimi was ringing from the hospital. There had been an accident. Even before he heard the news, he knew. It was Julia … .

She had said goodbye to Mimi that afternoon and started walking home.

She hadn't looked before she stepped out into the road. She didn't even see the car, and the driver wasn't able to stop in time.

The car had killed her immediately.

When he heard the news, John did not move. He couldn't breathe.

His mother was dead.

* * *

After the funeral, there was a wake* at Julia's house. The place was full of family, friends and neighbours. People stood in small groups and spoke quietly. John sat alone in the corner. Nothing seemed real to him. How could his mother be dead?

Above the sound of the quiet conversations around him, he heard a few notes from a banjo in the other room. A sudden anger ran through John. He ran into the other room and saw Paul with his mother's banjo.

'What is *this*?' shouted John. 'Band practice? I don't think so!'

He pulled the instrument out of Paul's hands and lifted

* A wake is a party for a person's family and friends to remember them after their funeral.

it over his head. He was going to hit it down onto the floor, but his old friend Pete reached for it. 'John, it's your mum's!'

'My mum's dead!' cried John, mad with pain and anger. Then he brought his head down, right into his old friend's face. Pete fell to the floor with his hands to his nose and John ran out of the room.

It was Paul who followed him out of the house. 'John!' He reached him at the front gate and stood right in front of him. 'You want to hit me, too?'

A wild look shone in John's eyes.

'Go on then,' said Paul.

John hit him, fast and hard and Paul was on the ground, blood around his mouth. John looked down at him.

'I … I'm sorry.' He pulled his friend back up to his feet and hugged him tight. All the pain came out, all the anger and tears that had been inside for so long. 'I was just getting to know her,' he cried.

'I know,' said Paul.

'She's never coming back.'

'No. No, she's not.'

When the two went back inside, Pete was still bleeding from his nose.

'I'm stupid,' said John. He put a hand on his old friend's shoulder. 'I'm sorry.'

Pete smiled through his tears. John turned to the rest of the band. His voice broke as he tried to speak. 'Right! Everybody stop crying! We're supposed to be a rock 'n' roll band!'

Everybody in the room was laughing and crying.

Bobby appeared at the door. 'John,' he said quietly. In his hand he had an envelope, which he handed to John.

'She was saving this for you,' Bobby said simply.

John opened the envelope and saw that it was full of money.

* * *

He knew exactly what he wanted to do with the money Julia had left him.

There was a little recording studio in the city centre. It wasn't anything grand, but local bands could pay to go there and make their own records. When the Quarrymen arrived, they were just one of several bands there that day.

They carried their instruments inside and paid the man in the studio. For him, this was just a normal work day. For John and the band, this was the start of everything: it was their chance to properly record a song for the first time.

The studio was quite small, with microphones and sound equipment everywhere. The band didn't have long to get ready, but they didn't need much time. After a few minutes, they began to play.

As he sang, John remembered Julia: she would have loved this. He almost felt as if he could see her now; in his mind, she was laughing and dancing to the music with him.

John poured his heart into the song. This was who he was now — the *nowhere boy* years were over.

EPILOGUE
August, 1960

John didn't live at Mimi's house anymore, but he still visited often. She might not actually say it, but John knew that Mimi was always happy to see him.

'Why didn't you telephone to say you were coming?' she asked now.

'Well, I don't have a phone.'

'Do you have anything useful in that hole you call a home?' She smiled at him. 'And what can I do for you today?'

'I'm going to Hamburg, Mimi,' John told her.

'Hamburg?' She sounded surprised.

'It's in Germany.'

Mimi gave him one of her looks.

'I'll be gone for a couple of months … maybe more.'

Mimi tried to look as if this didn't affect her. John knew better.

'And is this with the new group? What are they called again?'

'Do you care?' asked John. The Quarrymen had finished; now they were the Beatles.

Mimi just smiled. 'They all sound the same to me.'

Then John remembered why he had come. 'Have you got my birth certificate?' he asked. 'I need it for my passport.'

While Mimi got the certificate from upstairs, John looked around at the house that had been his home. He looked at the photos of himself as a child. He knew that Mimi would never take these down.

When Mimi returned, he handed her the passport form that he had to complete. 'Can you sign this?' he asked.

Mimi looked at the form carefully. 'Where do I sign?'

'Where it says Parent or Guardian,' John told her.

Mimi looked up. 'But which am I?'

That was easy. 'Both,' said John.

It wasn't often that Mimi reached out for a hug, but she hugged John now.

'Don't be silly,' he said with a half-smile. He gently stepped away and into the hall. It was time for him to go.

While he was putting his jacket on, Mimi came to the door. 'John?' She made two circles with her fingers and thumbs and held them up to her eyes. 'Glasses.'

As he'd done hundreds of times before, John took his glasses out of his pocket and put them on. 'I'll call you when I get to Hamburg, OK?'

'Don't forget,' said Mimi. Then with a nervous smile she added, 'Please.'

This was an important moment. In his heart, John knew that he wasn't just going away for a couple of months. It was bigger than that. For years this had been his home, and now he was really leaving.

He gave her a kiss and then walked towards the front door. As soon as he was outside, he took his glasses off and put them back in his pocket.

John called Mimi as soon as he arrived in Hamburg. He called her every week after that, for the rest of his life.

THE BEATLES

John Lennon became famous all around the world as one of the Beatles. In *Nowhere Boy*, fans will recognise some important moments in the band's early history.

MEETING WITH PAUL MCCARTNEY

Years later John spoke about his first meeting with Paul in July, 1957. He had been worried because Paul was clearly better on the guitar than he was.

Both John and Paul became brilliant songwriters. In the band's early years, they often worked together, but many of the songs were written by just one or the other. However, they were always credited to Lennon/McCartney.

ELVIS PRESLEY

John spoke about the effect that Elvis Presley had on him as a teenager. Later the Beatles met John's old hero. However, years after this, they learned that Elvis, was worried about the Beatles' success and had asked the US government to send the band back to the UK!

The Beatles in Hamburg in the early 1960s

HAMBURG

In the film, John tells Mimi the band is going to Hamburg. The Beatles returned to this German city often at the start of their career. They played in all-night bars and clubs, often for seven hours a night. John once said, 'I grew up in Hamburg, not Liverpool.'

> **Did you know …**
> **Guitarist George Harrison really did audition for the band by playing upstairs on a bus!**

The Beatles at the time of *Sergeant Pepper* From left to right: Paul, Ringo, John and George

NOWHERE BOY

The film's title comes from a John's 1965 song, 'Nowhere Man'. By this time, both he and Paul were exploring new musical styles and subjects. Some of John's songs like 'Nowhere Man' were quite dark.

> **The Beatles were one of the most successful bands ever. Why were they so popular, do you think?**

STRAWBERRY FIELDS

In the film, John cycles past the gate to a children's home called Strawberry Field. He later used this childhood memory in one of his best – and strangest – songs, 'Strawberry Fields Forever'. By this time, the band was experimenting more and more. In the same year, *Sergeant Pepper's Lonely Hearts Club Band* appeared; for many, this was the most important album of the 1960s.

> **What do these words mean? You can use a dictionary.**
> **hero   credit   audition   experiment   album**

LIFE AFTER

The Beatles' success in the 1960s was built on a balance between their different characters, especially John and Paul's. But that balance could not last forever. In the 1970s, John faced life after the Beatles.

John and Yoko campaigned against war

John and Yoko

In 1968, John's first marriage ended. He had fallen in love with an artist called Yoko Ono. She changed everything for John, and he often spoke of her as his teacher. But he was becoming less interested in being a Beatle. The band continued to record albums, but John later spoke of the start of the band's 'slow death' at this time. When the band finally split up in 1970, John said, 'It feels good.' He and Yoko decided to begin a new life in New York City. He left the UK, and never returned. In America, he and Yoko became interested in politics and campaigned for peace at the time of the Vietnam War.

Lennon in the 1970s

Some John's most personal songs were on his first album after the Beatles, *Plastic Ono Band.* In painful songs like 'My Mummy's Dead' and 'Mother' he sings about losing Julia at a young age.

The title song of the next album, *Imagine*,

THE BEATLES

John with Sean and Yoko

became one of John's most famous: this contained the singer's hopes that 'the world will live as one'. The album also included 'How Do You Sleep?', an angry attack on Paul McCartney. As time passed, the two became friendlier – Paul later visited John's New York apartment a few times – but they never wrote or recorded together again.

For about eighteen months in the 1970s, John and Yoko lived apart; John called this time his 'lost weekend'. When he and Yoko got together again, John decided not to make music for a few years. He stayed at home and looked after their son, Sean. In 1980, he returned to the studio to record *Double Fantasy*. Much of this album was about the happiness of family life.

A Violent End

On December 8th, John and Yoko were returning home to their apartment building. Mark Chapman, a young man with mental illness, was waiting with a gun. He shot John in the back and chest. John Lennon died later that night; he was just forty.

Today fans can visit part of Central Park in New York near where John lived. It is called Strawberry Fields in memory of John. In the middle of this area is a single word, the title of one of his most famous songs: 'Imagine'.

Strawberry Fields, Central Park

> **Many people think that neither John or Paul were as good after the Beatles. What do you think?**

> **What do these words mean? You can use a dictionary.**
> split up   campaign   apart   mental

LIVERPOOL

Liverpool Then

Liverpool has a long history as one of the country's biggest ports. At one time, 40% of the world's trade passed through Liverpool, and it was known as the 'city of ships'. In the twentieth century, many passenger ships also came to Liverpool. This mix of nationalities helped to shape the strong Liverpool accent, and perhaps the people's famous sense of humour, too.

Gradually the north-west of England became less important in world trade, and so did the port. The docks also suffered a lot of damage during World War II. In the 1950s, when *Nowhere Boy* takes place, the port was becoming less busy. In the 1970s and 1980s, Liverpool faced hard times: many people in the city did not have jobs.

Liverpool Now

Liverpool celebrated its 800th birthday in 2007, and today many of the city's problems are in the past. It is a lively city which thousands of tourists visit every year. The city has got two famous football clubs, and in 2008 it was named a European City of Culture. It has more museums and art galleries than any other British city outside London. The most famous of these is the Tate Liverpool, which you can find in the docks area.

The Beatles in Liverpool

It is impossible to forget the Beatles when you are in Liverpool. This begins as soon as visitors arrive at the city's airport – 'John Lennon International Airport'. Fans can see many of the places and things from the band's past:

John Lennon International Airport

Aunt Mimi's House

The Cavern Club

✷ You can visit the house in Woolton where John lived with his Aunt Mimi until he was twenty-three. In 2002 Yoko Ono bought the house and it was opened to the public the next year. Inside everything looks the same as it did when John lived there.

✷ The first Cavern Club, where the Beatles played Insert text 'in 1973', was pulled down. Later a second Cavern Club was built and today tourists can go and see the same kind of dark, underground club where the Beatles played.

> **Which places in your country are known for their music? Why is this?**

What do these words mean? You can use a dictionary.

public   port   humour   trade   damage   gallery   trade

CHAPTERS 1–2

Before you read

Use your dictionary for these questions.

1 Complete the sentences with these words.

docks fair funeral grave genius harmonica
hug nod pat ride sighed uniform

- **a)** When his grandfather died, there were a lot of people at the … .
- **b)** In the past, a lot of ships arrived at the city's … .
- **c)** Mozart was a musical … !
- **d)** She plays the … in a blues band.
- **e)** I always give my old friends a … when we meet.
- **f)** It's exciting! We're going to a … today!
- **g)** She didn't say yes but she gave a … of her head.
- **h)** Every month we put flowers on our grandmother's … .
- **i)** The students at that school have a dark blue … .
- **j)** When my dog behaves well, I give him a … on the head.
- **k)** I don't want to go on another … today. I don't feel very well.
- **l)** 'It's very bad news, I'm afraid,' he … .

2 Look at 'People and Places' on pages 4–5 and answer the questions.

- **a)** Who does John live with?
- **b)** Who is his real mother?
- **c)** Who is an ambitious young musician?
- **d)** Who is John's best friend?
- **e)** What do John's teacher's think about him?
- **f)** Why did people often go to Blackpool?

After you read

3 Answer the questions.

- **a)** What gift does George give to John?
- **b)** What does the head teacher think John will do in the future?
- **c)** Why is John left alone at the house?
- **d)** Who is the 'woman with red hair' at the funeral?
- **e)** How is Julia's house different from Mimi's?
- **f)** Where do Julia and John go?

4 What do you think?

a) Look at this sentence from page 13:
'Yes, the woman with red hair was his mother, but she hadn't been *Mum* to him for a long time … .'
What is the difference between 'mother' and '*Mum*' here?

b) At the end of Chapters 1 and 2, John remembers part of something that happened in Blackpool when he was a child. What happened, do you think?

5 Writing
Imagine you are John. Write in your diary after the day out in Blackpool. How do you feel about seeing your mother again?

CHAPTERS 3–4

Before you read

6 Match the words with the definitions.
banjo   chord   shrug   string   suspend   swap
a) a small movement of the shoulders
b) two or more musical notes played at the same time
c) to give something you have for something that someone else has
d) a long, thin part of a musical instrument that makes a sound
e) to stop someone from coming to school or work for a short time
f) a musical instrument

7 Guess the answers. Then read and check.
Will John tell his mother the truth about what happened at school? Will she help him?

After you read

8 Who says these things? Match the people and the sentences.

John   **a)** 'You can't just come round here like this, you know.'
Mimi   **b)** 'I don't even know when I want you back.'
Julia   **c)** 'Don't lie to me, John Lennon!'
Mr Pobjoy **d)** 'Be a friend.'
Bobby   **e)** 'If you're here, why not learn something?'

9 Find and correct the mistakes in these sentences.
   a) John steals money from a shop in the city centre.
   b) John burns the letter to Julia.
   c) Julia teaches John how to play the guitar.
   d) Mimi comes to Julia's house when she learns that John has stolen from shops in the city.
   e) John tells Mimi that he is going to be an actor.

10 Writing
   Imagine that you are the head teacher at John's school. Write the letter to John's aunt. Explain why you are suspending him.

CHAPTERS 5–6

Before you read

11 Circle the correct answers about a music concert.
   a) Who is on the *stage*?   the band   the crowd
   b) Who gives the *performance*?   the band   the crowd
   c) Who *cheers*?   the band   the crowd

12 What do you think?
   What will Mimi think of John's idea to start a rock 'n' roll group?

After you read

13 Put these events in the right order.
   a) John and Paul practise playing the guitar together.
   b) John tells his school friends that he's starting a band.
   c) A boy called Paul McCartney meets the band.
   d) John and Mimi go to buy a guitar.
   e) George Harrison joins the band.
   f) The band plays a concert at a village fair.
   g) John begins to write music.
   h) Julia gives John some money to buy his guitar back.

14 What do you think?
   Describe John's feelings about …
   a) the band.   **b)** Julia.   **c)** Paul.

15 Writing

Imagine that you work for a local newspaper. Write about the performance of the Quarrymen at Woolton village fair or at one of their later concerts.

CHAPTERS 7–8

Before you read

16 Can you think of three situations when people use *candles*?

17 Guess the answers. Then read and check.

Look at the title of Chapter 7 and at the pictures on pages 63 and 64. What do you think John learns about his past in these chapters?

After you read

18 Are these sentences true or false? Correct the false sentences.
  a) John is excited about the birthday party.
  b) Julia is talking to Bobby when John arrives at the party.
  c) John asks Julia where his real father is.
  d) Julia explains that she left John's father.
  e) Mimi makes a birthday dinner but John forgets about it.
  f) Mimi gives him an electric guitar for his birthday.
  g) John does not let Julia come inside Mimi's house.

19 Answer the questions.
  a) What new relative does John learn about?
  b) Why did Alf take John to Blackpool?
  c) Who did the boy choose to go with?
  d) Where does John sleep on the night he hears the truth about his past?
  e) Where is Mimi going with some flowers?
  f) What decision does John tell Mimi about at George's grave?

20 Writing

Write the rest of the conversation between Mimi and Julia when they meet at the end of Chapter 8.

CHAPTERS 9–EPILOGUE

Before you read

21 Complete the sentences with these words. You can use a dictionary.
certificate   guardian   studio
a) The band are going to record their next song in a … in London.
b) Her aunt became her … after the death of her parents.
c) You need to show your passport or birth … .

22 What do you think?
Look at the title of Chapter 9. Who is talking? Who are they talking about? What does this mean, do you think?

After you read

23 Answer these questions.
a) Where does John study after he has left school?
b) How does the relationship between Mimi and Julia change?
c) What is important about the song 'Hello, Little Girl'?
d) What accident happens to Julia?
e) How does John use the money from Julia?
f) Why does John need his birth certificate?

24 What do you think?
a) When Mimi asks where to sign the form, why is John's answer so important to Mimi?
b) How has the relationship between John and Mimi changed by the end of the book?

25 Writing
Imagine that you are writing a book about the history of The Beatles. Use what you have learned from *Nowhere Boy* to write two or three paragraphs about John Lennon's early life.